RAS (Reticular System

How to Use it for Your Highest Good.

RAS (Reticular Activating System: How to Use it for your Highest Good.

By: Sherry Lee
Version 1.1 ~January 2024
Published by Sherry Lee at KDP

All information in this book has been carefully researched and checked for factual accuracy. However, the author and publisher make no warranty, express or implied, that the information contained herein is appropriate for every individual, situation, or purpose and assume no responsibility for errors or omissions.

The reader assumes the risk and full responsibility for all actions. The author will not be held responsible for any loss or damage, whether consequential, incidental, special, or otherwise, that may result from the information presented in this book.

All images are free for use or purchased from stock photo sites or royalty-free for commercial use. I have relied on my own observations as well as many different sources for this book, and I have done my best to check facts and give credit where it is due. In the event that any material is used without proper permission, please contact me so that the oversight can be corrected.

TABLE OF CONTENTS.

INTRODUCTION.

Within the expansive domain of human consciousness resides a formidable neural apparatus, the Reticular Activating System (RAS), which manipulates our perceptions, experiences, and realities.

Although it plays an essential role in our daily lives, its existence and potential continue to elude many. This book explores the enigmatic nature of RAS, furnishing a fundamental comprehension of its complexities and the profound ramifications it influences our everyday lives.

A compact yet formidable entity known as the Reticular Activating System resides at the brain's core, nested within the medulla. The RAS, often compared to a gatekeeper, filters the immense quantity of stimuli that bombard our senses every moment.

It determines which information is admitted into our conscious awareness and which is relegated to the subconscious's background din. Gaining insight into this neural sentinel is comparable to seizing control of our reality; doing so grants us the ability to affect the fundamental structure of our being.

To fully grasp the importance of RAS, it is essential to explore its evolutionary roots. This book examines the evolutionary path that culminated in the formation of the RAS in Homo sapiens and the adaptive functions it serves.

Racial and evolutionary strategies (RAS) have significantly influenced how our species has navigated the world and evolved from the rudimentary survival instincts of our predecessors to the sophisticated cognitive processes of the contemporary human mind.

Amidst the rapid progression of the digital age, our sensibilities are overwhelmed with an unparalleled abundance of information. Personal interactions, social media, advertisements, and news inundate our senses to the point where they overpower our cognitive faculties.

Regarding this matter, RAS functions as an indispensable instrument, aiding us in navigating the inundation of information and directing our attention toward what is genuinely significant. This section delves into the operational mechanisms of RAS in the contemporary era, providing insight into its influence on our convictions, inclinations, and priorities.

Gaining knowledge regarding the presence and operation of RAS grants access to an ethereal domain of boundless opportunities. By gaining insight into the functioning of this neural filter, individuals can utilize its potential to improve diverse facets of existence.

This BOOK places significant emphasis on the profound capacity for conscious awareness to bring about change, urging readers to initiate a process of self-exploration and personal mastery by activating their RAS.

As we investigate RAS and its diverse impact, this book guides the subsequent chapters. Every segment of the book has been carefully constructed to offer comprehensive understandings, applicable methodologies, and tangible instances that demonstrate the implementation of RAS principles.

Through exploring manifestation, emotional intelligence, goal setting, and positive thinking, readers will thoroughly comprehend how RAS can be effectively employed to benefit others. Subsequent chapters will explore the intricacies of RAS in greater detail, revealing its concealed aspects and disclosing pragmatic approaches to utilize its potential effectively.

As a collective, we shall begin an enlightening expedition that will enable readers to attain their utmost capabilities and materialize their most profound aspirations through a comprehensive understanding of the Reticular Activating System.

Let's get started.

CHAPTER 1: RETICULAR ACTIVATING SYSTEM (RAS) AND ITS FUNCTIONS IN THE BRAIN.

The human brain controls our thoughts, emotions, and behaviors, an intricate neural network of billions of neurons. Central to this complex system resides a diminutive yet extraordinarily potent Reticular Activating System (RAS) segment.

Anatomy of the RAS.

The Reticular Formation, an intricate network of nuclei interconnected with diverse brain regions, is situated at a profound level within the brainstem. The Reticular Activating System, a collection of neural circuits that regulate arousal, attention, and consciousness, lies at the heart of this formation.

Although relatively diminutive in size, the RAS serves a critical function by filtering the constant deluge of sensory data that bombards our senses at any given instant. This enables us to concentrate on what is most vital.

Filtering of Information and Attention.

Information filtration is among the principal functions of RAS. Rapidly, our senses are bombarded with abundant stimuli, including sights, sounds, scents, and sensations. The RAS functions as a gatekeeper, filtering this sensory input selectively so that only a portion reaches our conscious mind. Survival-critical selective attention allows us to concentrate on vital information while disregarding extraneous background noise.

Also, RAS significantly influences our state of consciousness. It regulates our consciousness, spanning from wakefulness to different sleep phases. RAS maintains vigilance throughout the day, ensuring we remain responsive to our surroundings. RAS inhibits sensory input during sleep, enabling the brain to restore tissues, consolidate memories, and rejuvenate for the following day.

What mechanism does RAS exert its effects?

A hormone system, the Renin-Angiotensin System (RAS), is essential for regulating body fluid volume, electrolyte balance, and blood pressure. Renin, angiotensinogen, angiotensin-converting enzyme (ACE), angiotensin II, and angiotensin receptors are among its many constituents.

The RAS operates as follows:

Renin is an enzyme secreted by specialized renal cells in reaction to hypotension, hypovolemia, or sodium deprivation. Renin exerts its pharmacological effects on angiotensinogen, a liver-secreted protein that enters the circulation.

Angiotensinogen is a precursor protein secreted into the circulation after being produced by the liver.

Angiotensin I is produced when renin cleaves angiotensinogen.

Angiotensin I is comparatively dormant, as evaluated by Angiotensin-Converting Enzyme (ACE). By eliminating a dipeptide, ACE, predominantly present in the lungs, transforms angiotensin I into angiotensin II.

Angiotensin II functions as a highly effective vasoconstrictor, causing the constriction of blood vessels. As a consequence, blood pressure is elevated.

Also, it induces the secretion of aldosterone, a hormone that facilitates the renal reabsorption of sodium and water, thereby causing an augmentation in blood volume. Angiotensin II also promotes the production of antidiuretic hormone (ADH), thereby augmenting the process of water reabsorption in the renal system.

Angiotensin II interacts with distinct receptors (AT1 and AT2 receptors) located on cellular surfaces, notably in the brain, adrenal organs, and blood vessels. Angiotensin II induces a range of physiological responses upon binding to these receptors, including vasoconstriction, aldosterone secretion, and stimulation of thirst.

The RAS regulates blood pressure and electrolyte balance by controlling blood vessel constriction, blood volume, and sodium balance. This system can become dysregulated, which may result in hypertension and other cardiovascular complications. Many hypertension medications reduce blood pressure by inhibiting the activity of ACE or angiotensin II receptors, which are RAS targets.

What is the fight-or-flight activating system of the reticular system?

A vital brainstem component, the reticular activating system (RAS), controls arousal, sleep-wake cycles, and consciousness. Utilizing filtering and processing sensory data enables the brain to concentrate on pertinent stimuli while disregarding extraneous ones. The fight-or-flight response, a physiological reaction that transpires in reaction to a perceived threat or peril, is another mechanism in which the RAS is involved.

The hypothalamus gets a distress signal from the amygdala, a brain region responsible for emotional processing when an individual perceives a real or imagined threat. The hypothalamus releases stress hormones, including adrenaline and cortisol, to initiate the fight-or-flight response.

The body is prepared to combat or flee from the threat in response to these stress hormones. Fight-or-flight response-related physiological alterations include, among others, an elevated heart rate, accelerated respiration, dilated pupils, and increased blood flow to muscles. These alterations facilitate the body's prompt and efficient response in a potentially hazardous circumstance.

By augmenting sensory perception and alertness, the RAS contributes to this process, enabling an individual to react rapidly to the peril. It increases the individual's general state of arousal and facilitates concentration on the perceived threat by obstructing extraneous sensory data. This heightened vigilance and focus can be essential for survival in threatening situations.

In addition to exerting control over attention and consciousness, RAS profoundly affects our behavior. It reacts to internal and external events, influencing our environmental reactions.

RAS is a guiding light when we establish goals, directing our focus and effort toward resources and opportunities that align with those goals. This phenomenon elucidates why pertinent information and opportunities appear seemingly from nowhere after concentrating on a specific goal.

What function does RAS serve in awakening?

A complex network of brainstem nuclei and pathways, the Reticular Activating System (RAS) is essential for regulating arousal, wakefulness, and consciousness. It determines which incoming sensory stimuli merit attention and which should be disregarded by functioning as a filter. The RAS is implicated in a multitude of awakening and consciousness-related functions, which comprise:

Arousal: The RAS regulates the brain's wakefulness and general state of arousal. It filters internal signals and environmental sensory stimuli, enabling the brain to concentrate on vital information and maintain vigilance.

The RAS maintains a strong correlation with the sleep-wake cycle. Active and promoting alertness, the RAS is engaged during the awake state. The RAS experiences a reduction in activity during sleep, which facilitates the brain's progression through distinct stages of sleep.

Attention and Focus: By filtering out irrelevant stimuli, the RAS assists in directing attention and focusing. It enables the brain to ignore distractions to focus on particular duties or stimuli.

The RAS is a component in the process of consciousness maintenance. Alterations in the functioning of the RAS are hypothesized to result in altered states of consciousness, including coma and persistent vegetative states.

Stimulus Response: The RAS influences how the brain reacts to sensory stimuli like light, sound, and pain. It facilitates the processing and prioritization of these stimuli, enabling the brain to react suitably.

In brief, the RAS plays an essential role in regulating consciousness, attention, and arousal as a component of the brain's neural network, thereby significantly contributing to the awakening process and the maintenance of alertness and awareness.

Neural Pathways and Activation of the RAS.

Complex neural pathways facilitate RAS activation. Specific neural circuits linked to RAS are activated by goal-directed behavior or positive thinking. Neurotransmitters, including dopamine and norepinephrine, play critical roles in these processes.

Dopamine, often called the "feel-good" neurotransmitter, establishes a positive feedback loop that incentivizes individuals to strive for their goals by reinforcing actions that result in pleasure and reward.

Adaptability and Plasticity of RAS.

Significantly, RAS demonstrates plasticity, which enables it to reorganize and modify neural connections in response to stimuli and experiences. People can modify their RAS responses by engaging in deliberate activities such as mindfulness, visualization, and affirmations. A higher probability of attaining desired outcomes increases as neural pathways associated with positive thoughts and goals are fortified through consistent concentration.

Impact of Non - regulation of the RAS.

Interruptions in the functioning of the RAS can result in substantial ramifications. RAS non - non-regulation is associated with conditions including attention deficit disorders, insomnia, and specific neurological disorders. Gaining insight into the fundamental neural mechanisms can positively influence therapeutic interventions, instilling optimism in those afflicted with such conditions.

The Reticular Activating System, distinguished by its intricate neural circuitry and substantial influence on consciousness, attention, and behavior, is evidence of the brain's magnificence and complexity.

Exploring the scientific principles underlying RAS provides invaluable knowledge regarding the mechanisms that influence our reality. Equipped with this understanding, we can leverage the capabilities of RAS to effectuate profound personal changes, accomplish our goals, and attain our utmost capabilities.

CHAPTER 2: MAJOR FUNCTIONS OF THE RETICULAR ACTIVATING SYSTEM.

A complex neural network situated in the brainstem, the reticular activating system (RAS), is essential for modulating wakefulness, alertness, and consciousness. It functions as an information filter, distinguishing between stimuli that warrant attention and those that are disregarded.

The regulation of cortical arousal is a fundamental function of the RAS, which is also implicated in many physiological and psychological processes. This chapter will examine the three primary functions of the reticular activating system in depth.

1. Mechanisms Governing Wakefulness and Arousal:

An essential role of the reticular activating system is the regulation of wakefulness and arousal. In addition to functioning as a wakefulness center, the RAS regulates the transition from slumber to wakefulness.

The RAS reduces arousal levels and inhibits sensory input during sleep, allowing the body and brain to recover and rest. The RAS becomes more active as an individual awakens, resulting in heightened arousal and alertness.

Among the sensory systems that provide input to the RAS are vision, hearing, and touch. The organism analyses the sensory data and ascertains the optimal arousal required in the given circumstance.

For instance, when confronted with a difficult or menacing circumstance, the RAS heightens arousal to improve an individual's capacity to react promptly and efficiently. On the contrary, in tranquil and non-perilous circumstances, the RAS regulates its level of arousal to preserve energy.

2. Sensory Information Filtering:

The reticular activating system is also responsible for the critical function of filtering sensory information. Constantly, the environment provides the brain with abundant sensory input, including sights, sounds, scents, and tactile sensations. By acting as a filter, the RAS ensures that only vital and pertinent information reaches the conscious mind.

The filtration procedure is critical to prevent sensory overload and preserve concentration and attention. The RAS facilitates the prioritization of sensory input according to its importance, enabling people to focus on immediate duties and stimuli.

For example, when individuals are in a crowded and noisy environment, the RAS eliminates extraneous noises, enabling them to concentrate on critical conversations or signals.

3. Emotional and Cognitive Function Modulation:

The reticular activating system modulates Cognitive functions, emotions, arousal regulation, and sensory information filtering. Engaging in interactions with diverse brain regions implicated in memory, learning, and emotional processing impacts an individual's cognitive state and emotional experiences.

The limbic system, which is accountable for regulating emotions and emotional responses, is linked to the RAS. The RAS can affect emotional states, including anxiety, happiness, and stress, via these connections. Controlling the activity of various cortical regions also influences cognitive processes such as concentration, attention, and decision-making.

In addition, the circadian rhythms and sleep-wake cycle are influenced by the RAS, which regulates the duration and timing of wakefulness and sleep. Sleep disturbances resulting from RAS disruptions may manifest as excessive daytime lethargy or insomnia, which harm an individual's general health and cognitive abilities.

Fundamental functions of the reticular activating system include modulating cognitive functions and emotions, filtering sensory information, and regulating arousal. The complex interconnections of its neural network enable it to assimilate sensory stimuli, regulate wakefulness, and exert influence over diverse facets of human consciousness.

Knowledge about the operations of the reticular activating system is essential to grasp the intricacies of human brain behavior and function.

CHAPTER 3: THE INFLUENCE OF BELIEFS ON RAS RESPONSES.

Belief systems are fundamental components of the complex human mind, acting as the foundation upon which our thoughts, emotions, and behaviors are constructed. Gaining insight into the intricate relationship between belief systems and the Reticular Activating System (RAS) reveals the essential means by which we can maximize our capabilities and attain the utmost good.

Beliefs are profoundly held convictions concerning oneself, one's community, and the external environment. These beliefs ultimately determine our reality by shaping our perceptions and influencing our decisions.

The human mind is perpetually inundated with an impossible volume of information; beliefs function as filters, permitting specific information to traverse while impeding the transmission of others. In this context, RAS functions as the gatekeeper, reinforcing preexisting beliefs and correspondingly influencing our experiences.

RAS functions according to the concept of selective attention. The cognitive process regulates the inundation of sensory data by directing attention toward particular stimuli that corroborate our preexisting convictions.

For instance, RAS will obstruct potential opportunities from our vision field if we believe that such opportunities are limited in number. On the contrary, positive beliefs regarding abundance will result in RAS emphasizing opportunities consistent with said beliefs, thereby increasing their visibility and feasibility.

Limiting beliefs are convictions that are disempowering and impede one's progress and achievement. These beliefs often originate from adverse self-perceptions, previous experiences, or social conditioning.

Limiting beliefs often encountered encompass feelings of worthlessness, apprehension towards failure, and self-doubt. RAS reinforces negative thought patterns and self-destructive behaviors when influenced by these limiting beliefs; thus, it perpetuates a cycle of unrealized potential.

Identifying and confronting limiting beliefs are critical to effectively utilizing RAS for constructive change. By cultivating introspection and self-awareness, individuals can discern the origins of these beliefs.

Various strategies, including journaling, therapy, and positive affirmations, can be utilized to assist in the process of reframing these beliefs and substituting them with convictions that are constructive and empowering. As these empowering convictions become ingrained, RAS modifies its filtering mechanism, granting access to a world overflowing with potentialities.

Transforming the Brain:

The brain's extraordinary capacity to reorganize itself, known as neuroplasticity, is essential for reshaping beliefs and, by extension, RAS responses. Regular exposure to positive and affirming thoughts and experiences strengthens the neural pathways of empowering beliefs. RAS aligns naturally with these positive beliefs as these pathways become more robust, amplifying their influence on behavior and perception.

The development of empowering belief systems requires consistent and deliberate effort. Positive self-talk, visualization, and meditation are all effective techniques for reinforcing these beliefs. Increasing one's self-esteem through engagement in activities that provide support and companionship reinforces these empowering beliefs.

RAS develops an acute awareness of these favorable convictions as time passes, directing people toward opportunities, connections, and encounters that correspond with their recently acquired self-assurance and value.

Individuals' adoption of empowering beliefs has far-reaching transformative consequences that impact multiple facets of their lives. Enhanced professional opportunities, strengthened personal connections, and increased satisfaction are organic outcomes of this internal transformation.

Having become mindful of these empowering convictions, RAS consistently focuses on opportunities that foster individual and vocational development, thereby establishing a cycle of success and positivism that reinforces itself.

Fundamentally, the correlation between RAS and belief systems highlights the profound influence that our convictions and thoughts exert on the trajectory of our lives.

By acknowledging the influence of beliefs on Reticular Activating System (RAS) responses and proactively nurturing empowering convictions, people can optimize the functionality of their RAS, which will serve as a compass in their pursuit of prosperity, satisfaction, and boundless opportunities.

By harmonizing one's convictions with RAS, one attains the utmost good, and the journey towards it is profoundly transformative.

CHAPTER 4: METHODS FOR PROGRAMMING RAS TO PRODUCE DESIRED RESULTS.

The Reticular Activating System (RAS) functions as a formidable filter within the complex network of the human brain, sifting through the countless stimuli that bombard our senses continuously. This filter ascertains the significance and merit of the information that warrants our deliberate focus.

However, this filter can be consciously programmed and utilized to accomplish our innermost desires and aspirations, which is a fact that many individuals fail to recognize.

Comprehending the RAS Programming Structure.

1. The Power of Intention: The power of intention is fundamental to the programming of your RAS. Your

beliefs and thoughts function as the foundation for your experience. By establishing explicit intentions, one gives precise directives to their RAS, directing it toward opportunities, individuals, and experiences that follow their aspirations.

2. Affirmations: These positive statements can rewire the subconscious when repeated consistently. By selecting congruent affirmations, you can progressively alter your beliefs and perceptions by directing your RAS to concentrate on experiences that align with your goals and aspirations.

3. Visualization Techniques: When it comes to programming your RAS, visualization is a potent instrument. Your brain interprets evocative mental images of your goals as actual experiences, stimulating the RAS to pursue opportunities corresponding to your imagined reality. Mental rehearsal and guided imagery are methods that augment the efficacy of visualization.

4. Establishing specific, measurable, attainable, relevant, and time-bound SMART goals is essential to

effective goal formulation. The RAS can concentrate on the requisite actions and resources by establishing precise goals. Consistently evaluating your goals ensures that they remain in your consciousness and that your RAS remains tuned to pertinent prospects.

Strategies for Efficient RAS Programming.

1. Emotional Alignment: The programming of your RAS is heavily influenced by your emotions. Imbuing one's goals with positive emotions, including enthusiasm, delight, and appreciation, generates a formidable resonance that magnifies the consequences of one's intentions. The RAS is more strongly stimulated by emotionally charged goals, compelling it to seek experiences corresponding to emotional frequency.

2. Repetition and Consistency: To reprogram your RAS, consistency is vital. By reinforcing your intentions, repetition causes them to become ingrained in your subconscious.

By consistently applying positive affirmations, visualizations, and goal-related stimuli, one can fortify the neural pathways linked to the intended outcomes, thereby increasing the accessibility of said outcomes to the RAS.

3. Morning and Evening Routines: By integrating RAS programming techniques into your morning and evening routines, you can take advantage of the increased receptivity of the brain during these specific periods.

Enhancing the RAS programming process, beginning the day with positive affirmations and visualization, establishes a proactive tone while reflecting on your goals before bedtime and primes your subconscious mind to work on them during sleep.

4. Cultivating an attitude of gratitude can significantly enhance positive experiences. By incorporating a daily practice of gratitude into your life, you rewire your RAS to perceive and attract more things for which to be grateful, shifting your attention from scarcity to abundance. Gratitude for both present and

forthcoming bounties elevates the vibrational frequency of one's intentions, thereby fortifying their impact on the RAS.

Conquering Obstacles in RAS Programming

1. Confronting Limiting Beliefs: Limiting beliefs impede the seamless progression of RAS programming by functioning as barriers. Identifying and confronting these beliefs is critical to achieving successful RAS reprogramming.

Cognitive reframing and self-affirmations are two techniques that facilitate the deconstruction of limiting beliefs, thereby making way for empowering thoughts and intentions.

2. Persistence and patience: RAS programming is a gradual undertaking that demands perseverance and patience. Although instant results are uncommon, it is possible to gradually influence your RAS with consistent effort and unwavering confidence in your abilities. Have faith in the process, commemorate

minor accomplishments, and sustain a steadfast conviction in the efficacy of your intentions.

3. Adaptability and Course Correction: Throughout your RAS programming endeavors, you might confront unforeseen obstacles or modifications in your goals. Maintaining a flexible mindset and being receptive to adjustments in direction is imperative. Your RAS is adaptable to new desires and intentions so long as you consistently and transparently communicate your revised goals.

A journey of self-transformation, programming your RAS grants you the ability to direct your life and create your reality. By comprehending the complexities of the RAS and implementing time-tested methodologies, one can effectively utilize the complete capacity of one's mind to materialize one's ambitions and hopes with unwavering assurance.

As you further develop your RAS programming abilities, remember that your thoughts, beliefs, and intentions can manifest your desired life. Accept this influence and permit your RAS to direct you towards your utmost welfare.

CHAPTER 5: WHAT HAPPENS WHEN RAS IS PERPETUALLY ACTIVE AND DAMAGED?

The constant activity of the RAS can result in different complications and disturbances in normal brain function. Many potential repercussions may result from an overactive RAS.

Disruptions in Sleep: The RAS assists in the regulation of sleep-wake cycles. Constant activity may impede one's capacity to initiate or maintain sleep, potentially resulting in insomnia or other sleep-related ailments.

Hyperarousal: A constant alertness or hyperarousal may result from an overactive RAS. A condition of increased vigilance such as this may induce feelings of anxiety, restlessness, and trouble relaxing.

Difficulty Concentrating: Attention and focus are also processes regulated by the RAS. Persistency in physical activity can pose difficulties in maintaining focus and concentrating on tasks, resulting in reduced productivity and compromised cognitive abilities.

Stress and Anxiety: Anxiety and chronic stress may be exacerbated by an overactive RAS. Persistent irritation of the stress response can result in the development of emotions such as stress, unease, and persistent anxiety.

Physical Manifestations: Prolonged activation of the RAS may give rise to physiological manifestations, including tachycardia, muscular strain, and heightened arterial pressure. These symptoms may contribute to general discomfort and have adverse health effects.

Consequences for Mental Health: Extended periods of hyperactivity of the RAS have been associated with the development of anxiety disorders such as post-traumatic stress disorder, generalized anxiety disorder, and panic disorder.

It is critical to acknowledge that an excessively active RAS may arise from a multitude of factors, encompassing substance abuse, stress, trauma, or specific medical conditions.

Urgently consult a mental health specialist or healthcare professional if you suspect that someone you know is exhibiting symptoms consistent with an overactive esophageal system (RAS). Treatment alternatives may consist of medication, therapy, relaxation techniques, or lifestyle adjustments, contingent upon the etiology and intensity of the symptoms.

Damage to the reticular activating system.

A network of neurons in the brainstem, the reticular activating system (RAS), is vital for modulating arousal, attention, and sleep-wake cycles. The consequences of harm inflicted upon the reticular activating system are contingent upon its location and degree of injury. The following are some potential repercussions of RAS damage:

Coma: Severe injury to the RAS can induce a prolonged state of unconsciousness from which the individual can't be revived; this condition is known as a coma. Reduced awareness and responsiveness may ensue from impairment in the RAS, the nerve cell responsible for regulating consciousness and vigilance.

A disruption to the RAS may result in altered states of consciousness, including but not limited to bewilderment, disorientation, or drowsiness. It may be difficult for the individual to remain conscious and vigilant.

Sleep disturbances: The regulation of sleep-wake cycles is a function of the RAS. Normal sleep patterns may be disrupted by damage to this system, resulting in insomnia, excessive daytime drowsiness, or other sleep disorders.

Arousal and attention impairment: The RAS is vital for sustaining focus and attention. Impairment of this system may lead to difficulty sustaining focus and concentration and a propensity for easy diversion.

Attenuated reactivity to stimuli: The RAS processes and filters environmental sensory information. The occurrence of harm may result in diminished reactivity to sensory stimuli, impeding an individual's capacity to respond suitably to visual, auditory, or other sensory inputs.

Motor abnormalities may arise due to RAS injury, manifesting in specific instances as muscle weakness or challenges in movement coordination. These effects may impair an individual's capacity to carry out routine activities.

It is essential to acknowledge that the precise manifestations and levels of severity may differ significantly, contingent upon the location and extent of the injury within the reticular activating system.

Rehabilitation and therapy may be required to manage the effects of RAS damage, and the prognosis for recovery is contingent on the characteristics of the injury and the individual. Proficient healthcare practitioners, such as rehabilitation specialists and neurologists, administer treatment and care following the individual's particular requirements.

CHAPTER 6: EMPLOYING RAS TO SURMOUNT CHALLENGES AND MAINTAIN CONCENTRATION.

Establishing goals is an essential component of individual growth and accomplishment. By acting as a filter for the vast amount of information our brain receives, the Reticular Activating System (RAS) enables us to concentrate on what is pertinent to our goals and desires.

Before examining the correlation between RAS and goal setting, it is critical to grasp the foundational tenets that underpin successful goal setting. SMART goals are specific, measurable, attainable, pertinent, and time-bound. Your RAS becomes activated to identify opportunities and resources that align with your goal when you have a distinct, well-defined purpose.

RAS Filtering of Your Goals:

RAS is a gatekeeper, permitting information ingress that aligns with one's goals while obstructing extraneous stimuli. Your RAS sifts through the vast quantity of sensory inputs you receive daily and emphasizes the information and opportunities pertinent to your goal when you establish it.

Engaging in selective focus enhances one's awareness, thereby increasing receptivity to the environment, individuals, and resources that may be beneficial in attaining one's goals.

Visualization is a potent instrument utilized to program your RAS effectively. By generating a vivid mental image of your goal, you direct your RAS to identify favorable circumstances and opportunities to facilitate your progress. Engaging in consistent visualization exercises enhances the correlation between one's goals and RAS, increasing openness to opportunities that align with one's vision.

Positive affirmations are succinct declarations of optimism that mirror one's aspirations and goals. Your subconscious mind is influenced by consistently repeating these affirmations, which reprogram your RAS to concentrate on the positive aspects of your goals. By incorporating your goals into affirmations, you effectively communicate with your RAS, influencing your thoughts and actions to further your goals.

Attempts to achieve a specific goal are inevitably met with obstacles. RAS may function as an essential tool in facilitating the surmounting of challenges. By engaging in solution-oriented thinking and maintaining a positive attitude, you direct your RAS to pursue opportunities and resources that will assist you in overcoming obstacles. This procedure improves one's capacity for problem-solving and strengthens one's fortitude and resolve.

Establishing Long-Term Success Goals:

In addition to being essential for short-term accomplishments, RAS-driven goal formulation is also instrumental in ensuring long-term success. By consistently using positive thinking, affirmations, and visualization to reinforce your long-term goals, you maintain a highly calibrated RAS capable of identifying the incremental progress that leads to your ultimate vision. With unwavering determination, this sustained focus propels you towards your long-term goals.

The relationship between RAS and goal setting is closely intertwined with a growth mindset, which posits that commitment and effort can enhance intelligence and capabilities. One can strengthen one's growth mindset, which entails embracing challenges, deriving lessons from setbacks, and maintaining perseverance through applying RAS techniques.

This cognitive transformation enables one to establish lofty goals, secure in the knowledge that their RAS will assist in heightened consciousness and concentrated attention.

Understanding the interplay between RAS and goal setting is a paradigm shift. By effectively implementing the principles delineated in this chapter, one can leverage the capabilities of their Reticular Activating System to establish significant and attainable goals, surmount obstacles, and ultimately actualize their aspirations.

Remember that your RAS is an ally throughout your ongoing professional and personal development process, providing guidance and assistance in constructing a future predicated on your aspirations and potential.

CHAPTER 7: THE EFFECTS OF POSITIVE THOUGHTS ON RAS' RESPONSES.

Positive thinking is an influential force capable of profoundly altering the course of our existence. Within the Reticular Activating System (RAS) framework, positive thinking has a pivotal impact on cognitive processes such as information processing, reality perception, and response to diverse stimuli.

Positive thinking transcends transient moments of joy; it constitutes a way of life and an optimistic frame of mind. Positive thinking, at its essence, entails recalling the positive aspects of a given circumstance, anticipating favorable results, and having faith in one's capabilities to surmount obstacles. This mentality is the fundamental basis on which the Reticular Activating System functions at its highest level.

49

RAS: The Filter System of the Brain.

The Reticular Activating System is a filtration mechanism for the prodigious volume of information that constantly inundates the brain. It determines the relevance and necessity of information for our conscious awareness.

Positive thinking serves as a signal to the RAS, instructing it to prioritize constructive, empowering, and positive information. A positive attitude directs our receptive arousal system (RAS) to actively pursue favorable circumstances, resolutions, and experiences in the face of overwhelming stimuli.

The Impact of Positive Thinking on RAS Responses.

Due to selective attention, positive thinkers are more likely to observe and concentrate on the positive aspects of situations. A positive thinker is inclined to find the silver lining in difficult situations; the RAS amplifies this outlook, reinforcing the positive one.

Enhanced Resilience: Cultivating a positive mindset augments one's capacity to recover from adversities. By perceiving obstacles as transitory and surmountable, the RAS is stimulated to seek resolutions, thereby facilitating the navigation of challenges.

Positive thinkers tend to possess elevated self-esteem and self-assurance in their capabilities. These self-assured signals are detected by the RAS, resulting in a self-fulfilling prophecy in which confidence attracts favorable outcomes.

Optimism and Perspective: Positive thinkers maintain an optimistic outlook despite difficult circumstances. The RAS employs an optimistic outlook to discern information that strengthens hope, initiating a recurring pattern of favorable anticipations and encounters.

Strategies to Promote Positive Thinking and Augment RAS Activation.

Gratitude Practice: Positive thinking is enhanced by expressing gratitude for the positive aspects of life. Consistent gratitude practices prompt the RAS to focus on the bounty and favors, thereby establishing a constructive feedback mechanism.

Positive affirmations are highly effective mechanisms for altering thought processes. The RAS is activated by repeating positive self-statements and life affirmations; this reinforces the beliefs and attracts positive experiences in response.

Visualization techniques entail the formation of distinct mental images representing the intended results. By positively visualizing our goals and aspirations, the RAS becomes more receptive to opportunities and pathways that align with those goals.

Meditation on Mindfulness: The cultivation of awareness of the present moment devoid of judgment is facilitated by mindfulness practices. Through mindfulness, people can discern their thoughts and reroute detrimental thought patterns, enabling the RAS to concentrate on constructive and positive ideas.

The Effects of Positive Thinking on Well-Being as a Whole.

Physical Health: According to research, Positive thinkers have lower stress levels, a decreased risk of chronic diseases, and improved immune function. These wellness advantages are a result of the RAS's positive signaling.

Bettering one's mental and emotional health is correlated with reduced levels of anxiety and depression. By utilizing positive thinking to activate the RAS, individuals have the potential to enhance their mental and emotional resilience.

Positive thinkers often maintain healthier relationships due to their constructive mindset and capacity to perceive the positive qualities in others. Attuned to positive social interactions, the RAS fosters more satisfying relationships by fortifying the bonds between individuals.

Conquering Obstacles Utilizing Positive Thinking and RAS Alignment.

Challenge Reframing: Individuals with a positive outlook reframe obstacles as chances for personal development. Aligned with this viewpoint, the RAS proactively pursues resolutions and novel methodologies to surmount challenges.

A positive mindset is enhanced by cultivating a growth mindset, which views failures as valuable learning opportunities. The RAS encourages continuous improvement by emphasizing the lessons and insights from setbacks, supporting this transition.

The synergy between RAS and positive thinking exemplifies the transformative capacity of our beliefs. By adopting a positive outlook, we can consciously alter how our Reticular Activating System filters information, resulting in positive outcomes in many facets of life. Adopting a positive mindset enriches our encounters and fosters the development of a more harmonious and optimistic global community.

As our exploration of the complex mechanisms of the mind progresses, it is essential to bear in mind the immense influence that positive thinking, under the guidance of the RAS, can exert in molding a more promising and gratifying future.

CHAPTER 8: INFLUENCING RAS WITH VIVID MENTAL IMAGES.

Visualization is an influential cognitive process that generates distinct mental images through the mind's eye. Visualization is essential in maximizing the Reticular Activating System's (RAS) potential.

The underlying principle of visualization is that the brain cannot differentiate between actual and imagined experiences. Your brain interprets vibrant imagery as if it were a real event, activating comparable neural pathways and firing neurons in the same manner as it would during the physical experience. This phenomenon initiates the synergy that exists between RAS and visualization.

Processing the enormous quantity of information that our senses receive each second, the RAS functions as a filter. With intent and concentration, visualization sends a signal to the RAS, indicating that the image's subject is significant and deserving of attention.

By consistently visualizing particular goals, aspirations, or results, one can proficiently direct their RAS to focus on circumstances and prospects associated with those imagined desires.

Methods for Efficient Visualization.

1. Clarity and Detail: Your RAS is more significantly influenced by mental imagery that is more detailed and distinct. When visualizing, utilize every sense; consider what you perceive, hear, scent, taste, and feel. The visualization becomes more potent as the neural connections in the brain are fortified by the abundance of sensory data.

2. The incorporation of emotion enhances the complexity of one's visualizations. Commemorate not only the outcome but also the sentiments linked to attaining one's goals. Experience the delight, confidence, and contentment of having already achieved your goal. Emotional engagement heightens

the intensity of the emotional stimulus to which the RAS reacts.

3. Using consistent and repetitious visualization effectively communicates one's priorities to the RAS. Develop this into a habitual routine, ideally in a serene and concentrated setting. Your RAS will come to value your visualizations more often as you engage in their repetition; this will impact your perception and decision-making.

4. Positive Framing: Employ positive language to frame your visualizations. Reorient your attention to desired outcomes rather than fixating on what you wish to avoid. By evoking positive emotions, positive imagery reinforces the message to the RAS that these aspirations are advantageous and realizable.

The utilization of visualization in various domains of existence.

1. Professional Achievement: Conjure up an image of yourself achieving success in your vocation, such as

delivering an outstanding presentation, receiving commendation, or reaching noteworthy milestones.

Imagine the necessary actions to be taken and the competencies that require improvement. One can program their RAS to identify prospects for development and progression by engaging in success visualization.

2. Health and Wellness: Envision yourself in an ideal state of health through visualization. Envision yourself in optimal health, with your physical being mending, your vitality rising, and your overall state of being improving. This optimistic outlook can promote healthier behaviors, alleviate stress, and strengthen the immune system.

3. Relationships: Conjure images of harmonious friendships, familial bonds, and romantic partnerships. Visualize oneself engaging in effective communication, peacefully resolving conflicts, and receiving affection and support. By cultivating positive imagery, one can improve their interpersonal abilities and attract favorable relationships into their lives.

4. Conquering Obstacles: In the presence of challenges, engage in a positive self-image to envision one surmounting them with assurance and fortitude. Envision the obstacles diminishing in size when compared to your capabilities and resolve. Engaging in this mental image enhances one's self-assurance, facilitating the resolution of practical challenges.

Many success tales attest to the effectiveness of RAS alignment in conjunction with visualization. Artists envision producing masterpieces, entrepreneurs envision prosperous ventures, and athletes envision winning competitions. These individuals ultimately attain their goals by programming their RAS to identify opportunities, enhance their abilities, and surmount obstacles by consistently applying visualization techniques.

You can shape your reality through visualization by directing your thoughts, emotions, and actions. When combined with a comprehensive comprehension of the functioning of the Reticular Activating System, visualization gains an additional level of potency.

By capitalizing on the interplay between RAS and visualization, one can direct the mind toward desired outcomes, improve concentration, and materialize aspirational thoughts. By adhering to a systematic approach and having faith in the procedure, one can revolutionize one's life and attain the utmost welfare.

CHAPTER 9: MINDFULNESS PRACTICE FOR RAS AWARENESS ENHANCEMENT.

The concept of mindfulness, which entails being completely present and involved in the current instant, has garnered considerable attention recently due to its positive effects on mental, emotional, and physical well-being.

At its essence, mindfulness entails the intentional and non-judgmental observation of one's thoughts, emotions, and sensations. It involves being mindful of and completely embracing the present moment. Mindfulness practices often encompass body scan exercises, meditation, and profound breathing—each intended to foster presence and awareness.

A complex network of neurons in the medulla, the Reticular Activating System is essential for regulating wakefulness and alertness. It filters by determining which stimuli to prioritize and which to disregard. Regarding mindfulness, it is vital to comprehend how the RAS filters information.

The Point at Which RAS and Mindfulness Intersect:

Elevated Awareness: The mind is trained to be acutely aware of the present moment through mindfulness. Through the deliberate concentration of bodily sensations or respiration patterns, individuals can enhance their level of awareness. Under this heightened awareness, the RAS amplifies the experience of being present by filtering the information corresponding to the meditative state.

Emotional Regulation: Mindfulness enables people to observe their emotions impartially rather than becoming consumed by them. Emotional resilience is cultivated in individuals through consistent regimentation. The RAS reinforces a positive and tranquil state of mind by filtering stimuli that resonate with these balanced emotions and are attuned to the individual's emotional state.

Mindfulness meditation improves concentration by encouraging sustained attention to a particular object, which is often the breath. This extended period of focus enhances cognitive acuity and prolongs attention span. Under the influence of this heightened concentration, the RAS filters in information that promotes sustained focus, enabling people to maintain focus and engagement.

Attenuated Reactivity: Mindfulness instructs individuals to approach situations deliberately rather than impulsively. Individuals can regulate their responses by nonjudgmentally observing one's thoughts and emotions. Calibrated to this decreased reactivity, the RAS filters stimuli that encourage reflective responses, fostering composure and a sense of control.

Applications of RAS and Mindfulness in the Real World:

The integration of mindfulness principles into the decision-making process has the potential to result in more optimal choices. Through the practice of being entirely present, individuals can evaluate situations objectively.

This focused decision-making influences the RAS to filter information that supports rational choices, thereby facilitating the selection of alternatives consistent with one's values and goals.

Mindfulness has been found to improve both active listening and empathetic communication. Individuals can gain a deeper understanding of others by engaging in conversations with complete presence. Attuned to this mindful communication, the RAS filters in signals that promote genuine and positive interactions by facilitating meaningful connections.

MBSR: Mindfulness-Based Stress Reduction:

It has been scientifically demonstrated that mindfulness-based stress reduction programs, which integrate mindfulness practices and meditation, decrease stress, and enhance overall health. By filtering out stress-inducing stimuli, the RAS is stimulated by these stress-reduction techniques, which promote mental clarity and relaxation.

Conquering Obstacles and Fostering Harmony Between Mindfulness and RAS: Conquering Mind Wandering

Mindfulness practice presents the difficulty of contending with a wandering mind. When utilized efficiently, the RAS can redirect attention. One way to ensure sustained mindfulness is by employing techniques such as anchoring attention to the breath, which can aid in overcoming mind-wandering.

The cultivation of gratitude is a fundamental component of mindfulness, fostering an optimistic perspective on existence. The RAS, sensitive to positive emotions, selectively accepts opportunities and experiences corresponding to a grateful mindset, strengthening sentiments of gratitude and contentment.

Conclusion: In the intricate dance between mindfulness and the Reticular Activating System, individuals can discover a powerful tool for personal transformation and holistic well-being.

By comprehending the reciprocal relationship between mindfulness practices and the RAS, individuals can transcend their limitations and lead lives brimming with mindfulness, intention, and deep inner tranquility.

Adopting mindfulness as a lifestyle choice, with the backing of the RAS, provides access to a more profound and purposeful existence, where each moment is savored to its maximum potential.

CHAPTER 10: MANIFESTING DESIRES VIA RAS ALIGNMENT.

The skill of materializing one's thoughts and desires has been the subject of fascination among humanity for centuries: manifestation. Diverse techniques and methods have been investigated to manifest the desires, goals, and dreams of others.

As a fundamental principle of manifestation, the Law of Attraction states that what is like attracts that which is also. Similar energies are drawn into your life due to the vibrational frequency emitted by your thoughts and emotions. By acting as a filter, RAS magnifies experiences and thoughts consistent with your desires and beliefs.

Your efforts to manifest can be amplified by synchronizing your RAS with positive intentions. We underscore the significance of belief systems in this undertaking by examining empirical instances and scientific research that illustrates the interplay between RAS and the Law of Attraction.

Programming your RAS is comparable to coding the subconscious mind's operating system. This section offers pragmatic strategies and exercises to program your RAS for manifestation effectively.

You'll acquire practical techniques to enhance your capacity for manifestation, including constructing vision boards that promote RAS activation and the formulation of potent affirmations. By encouraging you to envision your desired outcomes vividly, guided visualization exercises increase your RAS's receptivity to these goals.

Transcending Constraining Beliefs: Unclogging the Way to Actualization.

A substantial impediment to the process of manifestation is the existence of constraining beliefs. These pervasive thoughts, often influenced by previous encounters or societal norms, function as obstacles to your aspirations.

Effective techniques for identifying, challenging, and replacing limiting beliefs are discussed in this chapter. Facilitating smooth manifestation requires reprogramming the subconscious mind and harmonizing one's beliefs with desired outcomes.

Emotions' Contribution to RAS-Driven Manifestation.

Emotions possess significant energetic influence over the activation and manifestation of the RAS. Gratitude, joy, and love are positive emotions that increase your vibrational frequency and attract experiences that align with them. On the contrary, adverse affective states such as fear and doubt have the potential to impede the transmission of energy for manifestation.

RAS and manifestation and provide strategies for fostering optimistic emotional states. Practicing mindfulness and gratitude exercises enables individuals to regulate their emotions, effectively augmenting their capacity for manifestation.

Rituals of Manifestation and RAS Alignment:

By acting as anchors for your manifestation practice, rituals, and routines, communicate to your subconscious mind that you are committed to achieving your goals.

Techniques for Advanced Manifestation: Quantum Physics and RAS:

The domain of quantum physics provides thought-provoking observations regarding the interdependence of celestial bodies and the influence of consciousness on the formation of reality.

The intersection between quantum physics, RAS, and manifestation is examined in this chapter. The observer effect and quantum entanglement illuminate consciousness's pervasive impact on the physical universe.

By incorporating these sophisticated principles alongside RAS techniques, one can enhance their manifestation practice to an unprecedented degree, thereby broadening the scope of potential outcomes and effecting concrete changes in reality.

You can manifest a life filled with prosperity, satisfaction, and delight by harmonizing your thoughts, emotions, and convictions with your aspirations. Embrace the potency of RAS, have faith in the manifestation process, and observe as your aspirations materialize before your very eyes. Commencing the process of manifesting one's highest benefit requires the deliberate engagement of one's Reticular Activating System.

CHAPTER 11: DEVELOPING EMOTIONAL INTELLIGENCE FOR RAS MASTERY.

Emotional intelligence (EI) pertains to the capacity to identify, comprehend, regulate, and proficiently employ one's emotions and those of others. Some essential elements constitute emotional intelligence, such as self-awareness, self-control, empathy, and social skills.

Self-awareness pertains to the capacity to identify and comprehend one's emotions, whereas self-regulation empowers one to govern emotions proficiently. Empathy facilitates the comprehension of others' emotions, while social skills equip individuals to navigate social situations adeptly.

Emotional responses are significantly influenced by the RAS, which filters and processes sensory information associated with emotions. The RAS interprets those emotions that we experience, including fear, happiness, and sadness, and subsequently influences our thoughts and actions. Enhancing our comprehension of the RAS's functioning in emotional circumstances can enable us to exert greater control over our emotions.

RAS-Mediated Development of Emotional Intelligence.

Self-Awareness and RAS: The initial stage in cultivating emotional intelligence involves attaining knowledge of our emotional impulses and patterns. We can gain greater control over our reactions by comprehending how particular stimuli stimulate our RAS and elicit emotions.

Self-Regulation and RAS: Emotion regulation can be aided by RAS programming techniques such as visualization and mindfulness. Through intentional mental and emotional redirection, regulating our emotional reactions and fostering emotional equilibrium is possible.

Empathy and RAS: To have empathy is to be able to comprehend the emotions of others. By facilitating the perception of non-verbal cues and affective signals, RAS improves our capacity for empathy. We can cultivate a more profound sense of empathy and connection with others by refining our RAS.

The cultivation of RAS awareness has the potential to enhance social interactions. Individuals can foster positive social experiences that fortify healthy emotional reactions through active participation and presence in social situations. Also, RAS techniques can assist us in more effectively navigating complex social dynamics.

Surmounting Emotional Obstacles Using RAS.

RAS and Stress Management: Emotional intelligence can be disrupted by chronic stress. By employing RAS techniques, such as positive affirmations and relaxation exercises, it is possible to alleviate stress responses and improve emotional regulation.

RAS and the Resolution of Conflicts: Conflicts often elicit intense emotions. Gaining insight into RAS in the context of conflicts can facilitate the regulation of emotions and the adoption of a composed and tranquil attitude when engaging in disputes. This consciousness may result in more productive resolutions.

By employing RAS techniques to cultivate emotional intelligence, individuals gain the ability to navigate the intricate nature of human emotions, thereby promoting improved interpersonal connections, efficient dialogue, and holistic emotional welfare.

By recognizing and capitalizing on the interplay between RAS and emotional intelligence, one can initiate a profound process of personal growth and attainment of emotional mastery.

CHAPTER 12: RAS AND ITS IMPORTANCE FOR PHYSICAL AND MENTAL HEALTH.

The correlation between health and the Reticular Activating System (RAS) is complex and profound. Our thoughts, beliefs, and general frame of mind profoundly influence our physical and mental health.

Comprehension of the Mind-Body Relationship.

The notion of the mind-body connection is widely recognized and accepted within the health and wellness field. Our emotional state and beliefs exert a direct influence on our physical well-being. Regarding the RAS, this correlation is strengthened.

By functioning as a filter, RAS permits specific information to enter our conscious awareness. Affirmations, positive thoughts, and positive beliefs can all stimulate the RAS in a manner that enhances vitality and health. In contrast, stress and negative thoughts can be detrimental to our well-being.

Function of RAS in hypertension.

The Renin-Angiotensin System (RAS) is an essential physiological component that maintains the body's fluid and electrolyte equilibrium and regulates blood pressure. It is a hormonal system that assists in regulating body fluid balance and blood pressure.

Describe how it operates:

Renin is an enzyme secreted by specialized renal cells in reaction to hypotension, hypovolemia, or sodium deprivation. Renin facilitates the conversion of angiotensinogen, a liver-produced protein, into angiotensin I.

Angiotensin I: Angiotensin-converting enzyme (ACE) catalyzes the conversion of angiotensin I to angiotensin II. Primarily, this conversion takes place in the airways. Angiotensin II increases blood pressure by constricting the blood vessels, as it is a potent vasoconstrictor.

Angiotensin II: Angiotensin II influences blood pressure through different physiological processes:

It increases blood pressure and peripheral resistance by constricting blood vessels.

It induces the secretion of aldosterone, a hormone responsible for facilitating sodium and water retention in the kidneys; consequently, this results in elevated blood pressure and volume.

It stimulates the secretion of antidiuretic hormones (ADH or vasopressin) and facilitates renal water retention.

The RAS facilitates anemia-induced reduction in blood pressure through vasoconstriction and angiogenesis. Conversely, hyperactivity of the RAS may contribute to the development of hypertension (high blood pressure), a risk factor for different cardiovascular diseases.

Antihypertensive drugs often employ angiotensin II receptor blockers (ARBs) and ACE inhibitors, which are RAS-targeting medications. By impeding the functionality of angiotensin-converting enzyme (ACE) or angiotensin II receptors, these medications induce vasodilation (blood vessel relaxation) and a reduction in blood pressure.

Individuals can optimize their health and well-being by implementing pain management techniques, understanding the mind-body connection, managing stress, enhancing immune function, adopting a positive lifestyle, and addressing chronic ailments. These actions collectively contribute to the potential of RAS.

As individuals become mindful of RAS's significant influence on their physical and mental well-being, they can adopt proactive measures to pursue a more robust and health-conscious existence.

CHAPTER 13: ENHANCING INTERPERSONAL CONNECTIONS VIA RAS AWARENESS.

Within the complex fabric of human existence, relationships serve as the vivid threads that interlace our individual experiences. Relationships profoundly affect our contentment and well-being, whether platonic, familial, romantic, or professional.

Relationships involve intricate interactions among feelings, beliefs, and behaviors. As a neural network in the brain, RAS significantly influences our emotional reactions and perceptions in interpersonal connections.

Emphasizing what is pertinent to our experiences and relationships filters the vast array of stimuli surrounding us. Through understanding this process, one can learn the underlying reasons for their attraction to particular individuals, circumstances, or actions.

Regarding RAS and Attraction:

Whoever we find alluring and appealing is influenced by RAS. Applying internal beliefs and desires to external signals directs us toward individuals whose qualities correspond to our subconscious preferences.

Programming our RAS can increase our awareness of the characteristics of our ideal partner, thereby facilitating the formation and maintenance of satisfying relationships.

Connection and Communication:

Successful communication serves as the fundamental building block for thriving interpersonal connections. RAS impacts our capacity for empathy, comprehension, and attentiveness.

By refining these capabilities via RAS techniques, we augment our aptitude for establishing profound connections with others. RAS awareness enhances the ability to engage in active listening, cultivating trust and emotional closeness within interpersonal connections.

Overcoming Obstacles in Relationships:

Every relationship confronts obstacles, such as miscommunications and disputes. By instilling in us the qualities of resilience and adaptability, RAS programming empowers us to navigate these challenges effectively.

Adopting a constructive outlook and confronting detrimental convictions makes it possible to convert conflicts into occasions for development, thereby fortifying the connections with our cherished ones.

Development of Intimacy and Trust:

Intimacy and trust form the foundation of significant relationships. Under the influence of prior experiences and beliefs, RAS has the potential to either foster or impede these vital components.

Recognizing and reprograming constraining beliefs creates an environment conducive to developing trust. Emotional and physical intimacy is enhanced when RAS is in harmony with vulnerability, honesty, and authentic connection.

Professional Relationships Using RAS:

In addition to influencing intimate relationships, RAS also impacts our professional interactions. Gaining insight into the significance of RAS in partnership, cooperation, and guidance amplifies our efficacy within the professional environment. By cultivating favorable perceptions of one's superiors and peers, one can establish a harmonious professional setting conducive to increased output and novel ideas.

Fostering Compassion and Empathy:

Compassion and empathy are essential qualities for fostering meaningful relationships. By enhancing these attributes, RAS programming empowers individuals to perceive the emotions of others and reciprocate with authentic benevolence more acutely. By incorporating RAS techniques that promote empathy and compassion, our interpersonal connections are enhanced, thereby nurturing a sense of camaraderie and assistance.

Within the domain of interpersonal connections, RAS functions as a catalyst and a guide. By comprehending its complexities and capitalizing on its potential, we alter our perceptions of others and improve our interpersonal connections, interactions, and overall relationship well-being.

CHAPTER 14: UTILIZING RAS PROGRAMMING TO CONQUER A SCARCITY MINDSET.

Achieving financial abundance is an aspiration shared by many individuals. Comprehending the function of the Reticular Activating System (RAS) can significantly impact one's quest for prosperity.

At its foundation, the RAS is a potent brain filter that determines which information is pertinent and significant. The RAS significantly influences the formation of our financial-related beliefs, attitudes, and behaviors. Gaining comprehension of this mechanism can enable individuals to reconfigure their financial circumstances.

Positive programming is an integral component when utilizing RAS to achieve financial abundance. One can reprogram the RAS to concentrate on opportunities and possibilities by ingesting positive thoughts, beliefs, and affirmations about prosperity and abundance. A positive perspective generates an attractive force that draws in financial success.

Money-related limiting beliefs are prevalent among individuals, often stemming from societal conditioning or early life experiences. RAS can greatly assist by identifying these beliefs and substituting them with empowering ones.

Strategies such as positive affirmations and visualization can assist in rewriting subconscious scripts concerning money, thereby creating an environment conducive to attracting abundance.

Determining and Attaining Financial Goals.

RAS can facilitate the endeavor of establishing and attaining financial goals. By establishing unambiguous financial goals, your RAS can exert ceaseless effort in bringing pertinent opportunities and resources to your attention.

Rational Attraction and the Law of Attraction.

The universal principle of attraction, known as the Law of Attraction, demonstrates a seamless alignment with RAS. Reinforcing one's RAS through visualization and conviction in one's financial goals enhances concentration and heightens sensitivity to opportunities that align with those aspirations.

Development of an Abundance Mindset.

In addition to material possessions, an abundance mindset constitutes a fundamental element of achieving financial prosperity. RAS can aid in developing this perspective by encouraging you to value the prosperity you currently possess, regardless of its magnitude.

RAS and Financial Decision Making.

RAS affects how funds are acquired, their management, and their investment. Refining your RAS can improve financial decision-making, identify lucrative investment opportunities, and avoid unnecessary risks. This section offers pragmatic advice on how to improve one's financial acumen by becoming knowledgeable about RAS.

Engaging in gratitude rituals and constructing vision boards are practical exercises that activate and program the RAS for long-term financial success.

By capitalizing on the potential of RAS to generate financial prosperity, individuals can alter their perception of money, unveil latent prospects, and actualize their most profound financial aspirations. Upon implementing the principles in this chapter, individuals may initiate a profound and life-altering expedition to pursue wealth and prosperity.

CHAPTER 15: ACTIVATING RAS TO UNLOCK CREATIVE POTENTIAL.

The criterion upon which innovation, artistry, and problem-solving all rest is creativity. It is the capacity to conceive novel possibilities, consider unconventional ideas, and implement distinctive concepts. This chapter will explore the intriguing correlation between creativity and the Reticular Activating System (RAS).

Creativity prevails in all facets of human existence and is not restricted to music and art. Creativity is essential for individuals across various domains, including science (e.g., investigators of novel phenomena) and business (e.g., authors of captivating narratives). It requires establishing connections between seemingly unrelated concepts, embracing the unknown, and thinking beyond conventional boundaries.

Innovative thought is heavily reliant on the Reticular Activating System. The RAS regulates the inundation of information the brain receives, enabling it to concentrate on particular stimuli while disregarding extraneous particulars.

In creativity, this filtering mechanism may serve as a constraint or a benefit. Gaining insight into the information filtering process employed by RAS empowers us to regulate and broaden our creative cognition.

Limiting beliefs—self-imposed barriers that impede imagination—are among the most significant impediments to creativity. Our beliefs strongly influence RAS, shaping our perception of reality according to our preconceived notions of possibility.

By recognizing and questioning these constraining beliefs, we can rewire our RAS to unleash an abundance of creativity. Positive affirmations and visualization are two such techniques that can be extremely useful in this endeavor.

Strategies Employed by RAS to Augment Creativity.

The cultivation of mindfulness facilitates an individual's capacity to be completely engrossed in the creative process, thereby fostering a more profound resonance with their thoughts and environment. This increased level of consciousness fosters innovative inspiration.

Participating in exercises that foster divergent thinking, such as collaborative ideation sessions and mind mapping, can assist in circumventing the RAS filter and facilitate the emergence of numerous ideas.

Implementing guided visualization techniques enables individuals to envision innovative problem-solving scenarios, thereby fostering creative solutions. This stimulates the RAS to concentrate on developing novel solutions, resulting in inventive breakthroughs.

Learning and Acceptance of Failure: RAS can be programmed to view failures as chances for development. Embracing setbacks as opportunities for growth and development fosters a spirit of venturelism and innovative exploration.

States of RAS and Creative Flow.

Enhanced creative flow states, distinguished by profound concentration, increased focus, and a perception of eternity, happen when RAS is in harmony with creative intentions.

Facilitating these states with strategies such as positive reinforcement, establishing explicit creative goals, and sustaining a conducive environment can enable creative individuals to attain their utmost potential.

Exploring the dynamic relationship between RAS and creativity reveals infinite potential outcomes. Individuals can access their latent creative abilities by acquiring programming expertise and effectively utilizing RAS capabilities. Embracing creativity enhances individual lives and propels societal advancement by nurturing innovation and molding a future brimming with imaginative marvels.

Remember, as you progress along your creative path, that the means to access creativity is intrinsic – it resides in your thoughts, convictions, and capacity to utilize the phenomenal potential of the Reticular Activating System.

CHAPTER 16: OVERCOMING ADVERSITY WITH RAS RESILIENCE.

Comprehending the Reticular Activating System (RAS) pertains not only to capitalizing on its potential for individual aspirations and triumph but also to surmounting the formidable obstacles that arise throughout one's existence.

The RAS, situated in the medulla, filters the enormous quantity of information that the brain receives daily. During periods of adversity, the RAS significantly influences our perception and concentration. By gaining this understanding, individuals can consciously direct their RAS to concentrate on solutions instead of problems.

Resilience is the mental fortitude required to recover from adversity; RAS can be a potent asset in fostering this quality. One common consequence of facing challenges is the development of negative emotions and limiting beliefs.

RAS can assist in reframing such pessimistic viewpoints. Individuals can cultivate a more optimistic perspective, even when confronted with challenges, by deliberately programming positive thoughts and beliefs into their RAS responses.

Fear and apprehension have the potential to immobilize individuals when confronted with obstacles. Even in challenging circumstances, individuals can develop a sense of composure and assurance through reprogramming the RAS.

Determining precise goals is critical in surmounting obstacles. Concentration and resolve can be enhanced by programmatically aligning RAS with these goals. Failures provide invaluable opportunities for growth and development. By utilizing RAS, one can foster a growth mindset in which setbacks are perceived as chances for development and acquiring knowledge.

By using positive RAS programming to reframe failures, individuals can recover more robustly, equipped with renewed insight and resolve.

Gratitude is an exceptionally potent sentiment capable of altering our perception of obstacles. Individuals can program their RAS to concentrate on the positive facets of their lives, even amid adversity, through gratitude.

When confronted with obstacles, the Reticular Activating System can serve as a beacon of guidance, shedding light on the trajectory towards perseverance, development, and success.

CHAPTER 17: RAS AND THEIR RELATION TO INTUITION AND GUT FEELINGS.

Within human consciousness, intuition exists as an enigmatic yet potent entity, subtly directing us through the unpredictability of existence. The relationship between intuition and the Reticular Activating System (RAS) reveals a captivating interplay between spirituality and neuroscience.

Constantly referred to as our gut feeling or inner knowledge, intuition is a type of unconscious reasoning. It is the inexplicable perception of whether something is correct or incorrect without concrete evidence to substantiate the sentiment.

Prevalent among the faculties of intuition are experiences, emotions, and subconscious knowledge that transcend the boundaries of logic. In contrast to deliberate cognitive processes, intuition functions rapidly, furnishing immediate understandings and direction.

Central to the complex network of the brain resides the Reticular Activating System, an information-filtering and processing neural structure. This chapter investigates the role of the RAS as the gateway to intuition.

The RAS determines which information attains our conscious awareness by utilizing its capacity to filter immense quantities of sensory input. It amplifies signals consistent with our beliefs, values, and priorities through this selective process. The filtering mentioned above mechanism is essential in augmenting intuitive capabilities.

RAS and Intuition: A Mutually Beneficial Relationship.

Symbiotic is the relationship between intuition and the RAS. Intuition subconsciously transmits signals to the RAS, directing attention to particular stimuli.

The reinforcement of intuition and confidence in it impacts the RAS's ability to prioritize pertinent information, enhancing our capacity to discern nuanced signals, patterns, and prospects consistent with our intuitive understandings. Consequently, the RAS enhances intuition, enabling individuals to differentiate authentic, intuitive prompts from superfluous cacophony or wishful thinking.

Developing Intuition via Activation of the RAS.

Understanding the reciprocal relationship between intuition and the RAS enables individuals to develop and improve their intuitive capabilities deliberately.

Methods such as visualization, meditation, and mindfulness significantly activate the RAS and refine its connection with intuition. Through the relaxation of the conscious mind, these exercises facilitate the RAS's ability to magnify intuitive signals, thereby granting individuals access to profound insights and wisdom.

Placing Trust in Intuition: Conquering Skepticism and Doubt.

One of the primary obstacles in effectively utilizing intuition's capabilities is surmounting skepticism and doubt. In contemporary society, rationality and evidence-based reasoning are often esteemed above intuitive guidance, which is dismissed as superstitious.

Through the recognition and validation of intuitive insights, individuals can fortify their rapport with the RAS, thereby attaining intuitive guidance that is more precise and dependable.

Problem-Solving and Decision Making Based on Intuition.

The function of intuition in decision-making is essential, as it directs individuals towards options consistent with their true identities and long-term goals. By synthesizing intuitive insights and logical reasoning, individuals can arrive at informed decisions that follow their innermost truth.

By developing an awareness of, confidence in, and proficiency with our intuitive faculties, we can harness the potential of the RAS to navigate the intricacies of existence with assurance and transparency.

By acknowledging intuition as a valuable facet of our awareness, we begin a profound and transformative expedition, propelled and augmented by the extraordinary functionalities of the Reticular Activating System, guided by the innate wisdom that resides within.

CHAPTER 18: ACHIEVING INNER HARMONY BY ALIGNING RAS WITH SPIRITUAL BELIEFS.

Within the expansive realm of human cognition, spirituality functions as an illuminating beacon, directing one toward self-exploration, inner tranquility, and a more profound comprehension of life.

The Reticular Activating System (RAS), an intrinsic neural network situated in the brain, substantially influences the formation of our spiritual beliefs and experiences.

Spirituality fundamentally surpasses the confines of structured religious institutions. It comprises the pursuit of significance, intention, and a deep-seated rapport with a force surpassing individual existence.

Spiritual encounters, including but not limited to contemplative practices, rituals, prayer, and meditation, are pursued by individuals in search of solace, wisdom, and a sense of belonging in the cosmos.

Operating as a gateway, the Reticular Activating System filters the immense quantity of information that the brain processes daily. RAS filters our perceptions within the context of spirituality, enabling us to concentrate on aspects consistent with our intentions, experiences, and beliefs. This filtration process impacts how we perceive signs, interpret spiritual encounters, and derive significance from existence's transcendent and mystical elements.

RAS's Function in Belief Systems.

Our RAS programming is profoundly imbued with our spiritual convictions. Our RAS will selectively filter information corroborating our long-held convictions regarding a higher power, consciousness, or energy.

As a result, individuals holding distinct spiritual convictions may construe an identical experience in various ways, demonstrating the subjectivity and malleability of the human psyche within the realm of spiritual matters.

RAS and the Practice of Meditation.

A fundamental spiritual practice, meditation, interacts directly with RAS. An individual's RAS programming can be altered through mindfulness and intense concentration.

By diligently engaging in meditation, individuals can develop their RAS to heighten consciousness, improve intuition, and grant access to profound spiritual insights. Transformational spiritual experiences, such as moments of illumination, unity consciousness, and spiritual awakening, may result from this RAS reprogramming process.

The Synchronicity and RAS.

Meaningful coincidences commonly describe synchronicity, a conduit between the material and spiritual realms. Synchronicity recognition and interpretation are functions of RAS.

A RAS tuned to a person's spiritual beliefs discerns events, symbols, and patterns that correspond to the individual's spiritual journey. Recognizing and embracing synchronicities can strengthen an individual's spiritual convictions and reinforce all entities' interdependence.

Trust, RAS, and Faith.

Trust and faith are fundamental components of the spiritual life. RAS affects our capacity to have faith and trust in the unseen, the unknown, and the divine; our beliefs influence it.

Gaining insight into how RAS evaluates faith-related information can enable individuals to fortify their spiritual beliefs, surmount uncertainties, and nurture steadfast confidence in their spiritual journey.

The profound correlation between spirituality and RAS underscores the intricate interplay between the human intellect and the sacred domain. Through examining this correlation, individuals can acquire a more profound understanding of their spiritual encounters, convictions, and the profound impact that can result from harmonizing RAS with their spiritual odyssey.

By recognizing the interrelation between RAS and spirituality, one can access a realm of inner tranquility, personal development, and a symbiotic relationship with the cosmos; this motivates readers to begin a profound quest for knowledge and spiritual enlightenment.

CHAPTER 19: UTILIZING RAS PRINCIPLES TO CREATE AN ENDURING IMPACT ON THE WORLD.

Within the vast fabric of human existence, the notion of legacy carries substantial weight. Beyond material possessions, a legacy comprises our constructive influence on others, the beneficial transformations we motivate, and the enduring impacts we fashion in the world. As an intermediary between the conscious and subliminal hemispheres, the Reticular Activating System (RAS) significantly influences our enduring impact.

Comprehending Legacy Via RAS:

1. The Significance of Intention: Intention is the foundation of RAS-driven legacy. By formulating

explicit and optimistic intentions, our receptive-aware system (RAS) discerns and concentrates on opportunities following those intentions.

By directing our thoughts and feelings towards establishing a beneficial heritage, we can motivate our RAS to identify and capitalize on prospects that benefit the collective welfare.

2. The Role of Altruism and RAS: Altruistic behaviors, motivated by compassion and empathy, significantly impact our RAS. Generosity and acts of compassion elicit positive emotions and cascade impact on society. The RAS phenomenon enhances our consciousness regarding the consequences of charitable deeds, strengthening our propensity for benevolent behavior.

3. Motivating Others: RAS transcends individual experiences and permeates the collective consciousness. By motivating individuals through our actions, accomplishments, and optimistic outlook, we initiate a cascade of events. The admiration and inspiration we bestow upon others endure beyond our demise as a portion of our legacy.

4. Empowering and Educating: RAS-led education enables individuals to pursue their aspirations and significantly contribute to society. By disseminating knowledge, expertise, and optimism, we augment the combined capabilities of the human race. By filtering in the information required for development and learning, RAS transforms education into a potent instrument for establishing a positive legacy.

5. Innovation and Creativity: RAS actively pursues opportunities and innovative solutions in response to innovation and creativity. By transcending traditional limitations, innovators effectively utilize the innovative potential of their RAS.

Promoting innovation facilitates the emergence of groundbreaking developments that can revolutionize lives and permanently alter the trajectory of history.

In Practice the RAS-Driven Legacy:

1. Philanthropy and Social Impact: Philanthropists guided by RAS are conscious of the profound

influence their contributions can exert on many causes. By directing their efforts towards improving society, they can utilize their RAS to recognize organizations and initiatives that effectuate sustainable social transformation. The communities they elevate and the lives they are better enduring are testaments to their legacy.

2. Environmental Stewardship: Individuals dedicated to the preservation and long-term viability of the environment recognize the interdependence of all organisms.

Environmentalists motivated by RAS acknowledge the critical nature of their mission and direct their efforts toward endeavors that safeguard our planet. By their endeavors, they ensure that future generations inherit a sustainable future and an ecological equilibrium.

3. Fostering Social Harmony and Peace: RAS enhances the influence of peacebuilders and proponents of social harmony. These individuals constructively impact their communities by

cultivating comprehension, acceptance, and compassion.

Peace initiatives spearheaded by the RAS establish a lasting heritage of solidarity, inclusivity, and reciprocal regard, cultivating a milieu in which disputes are resolved via discourse and collaboration.

4. Cultural Preservation: Individuals dedicated to cultural preservation protect heritage, languages, and customs. Recognizing the significance of cultural identity, RAS guides these individuals as they strive to safeguard the extensive fabric of human history. By promoting global unity in the face of diversity, their legacy endures through cultivating appreciation and comprehension of various cultures.

RAS and Individual Legacy:

1. Introspection and Development:

Utilizing RAS-driven self-reflection, people can identify their strengths, limitations, and opportunities for development. Individuals who deliberately direct their intentions towards self-improvement establish a lasting impact on their character and conduct, characterized by ongoing development and fortitude.

2. Family and Relationships: The influence of RAS on family dynamics and relationships is fundamental. Individuals establish a heritage of emotional stability and cohesion within the family unit by cultivating affection, comprehension, and assistance. Empathy and communication motivated by RAS reinforce connections, guaranteeing that the heritage of affection endures across generations.

3. Depicting Exemplars: Visionary leaders, under the guidance of their RAS, establish models for subordinates to emulate. These individuals motivate and instruct their followers by displaying integrity, determination, and ethical decision-making, imparting a lasting heritage of moral leadership. RAS-driven executives inspire and motivate their teams, enabling them to accomplish extraordinary accomplishments.

The Reticular Activating System is a guiding mechanism within the legacy domain, magnifying our motives and deeds. By comprehending the complex correlation between RAS and legacy, individuals can intentionally guide their thoughts and actions to generate a constructive and lasting influence on the global stage.

By utilizing the capabilities of RAS to mold our heritage, we begin a profound and impactful expedition, bequeathing a heritage that resonates throughout successive generations and motivates a future characterized by empathy, sagacity, and limitless possibility.

CONCLUSION.

Within the expansive fabric of self-exploration and individual metamorphosis, the Reticular Activating System (RAS) manifests as an illuminating beacon, providing direction toward our utmost welfare.

During this illuminating expedition, we have extensively examined the complex mechanisms of the human psyche, investigating the profound influence that RAS exerts on our cognition, convictions, affect, and behavior.

As this paradigm-shifting investigation nears its conclusion, it is critical to pause and contemplate the immeasurable knowledge acquired and the boundless opportunities that await.

Fundamental to our comprehension is the acknowledgment that RAS mastery is a functional, life-transforming instrument and not merely a theoretical concept. This understanding allows you to manipulate your existence, mold your fate, and actualize your most profound aspirations.

The expedition doesn't reach its culmination at this juncture; rather, it signifies an emerging phase in which you assume control of your life with renewed assurance and intention.

It was essential to comprehend how belief systems impacted RAS. Identifying and reshaping limiting beliefs can redefine one's self-concept and establish a more constructive and expansive reality.

You have developed and refined your emotional intelligence by acknowledging the relationship between emotions and RAS. Developing this consciousness not only improves one's emotional state but also refines the responses of the RAS, guaranteeing that they are following the utmost good. Through mindfulness, one can tune in to one's intuition, thereby permitting it to direct one's RAS responses and steer one towards choices consistent with one's genuine self.

By harmonizing your RAS with your spiritual convictions, you have adopted a comprehensive methodology towards individual development, fostering the development of your psyche while effecting change in your physical environment.

Remember, as you begin the subsequent stage of your expedition, that RAS mastery is a continuous undertaking. Rather than fixating on reaching a specific endpoint, one should embrace the perpetual transformation of one's thoughts, beliefs, and behaviors. In the following methods, you can further incorporate RAS wisdom into your daily life:

Develop daily practices that strengthen positive RAS programming. Engaging in morning affirmations, meditation, or visualization exercises are all effective methods to maintain a highly tuned and responsive RAS in pursuit of one's goals.

Reflect on your beliefs, desires, and experiences regularly. Determine whether any recurring patterns are following your utmost welfare. Modify your RAS programming accordingly to ensure it remains in harmony with your ever-changing ambitions.

Accept gratitude into your daily existence. Appreciating and acknowledging the blessings in one's life enhances positive RAS responses, thereby increasing the attraction of that which one is appreciative of. Develop an optimistic frame of mind, even when confronted with difficult circumstances, to maximize the benefits of your RAS.

As you venture into the limitless domain of your capabilities, bear the knowledge and insights of RAS. Permit it to be your guiding light, shining through the most ominous circumstances.

Accept the obstacles as chances for personal development, the regressions as preparatory stages towards achieving your aspirations, and the successes as symbolic milestones along an endless path.

Remember that you can design your reality and that RAS represents your most effective instrument. One can accomplish anything with intention, resolve, and steadfast confidence in their abilities. May the trajectory you forge towards your utmost good serve as a testament to the profound impact that RAS can have on your life.

This represents a fresh start—an emerging phase in which you assume the role of the prodigy, the architect, and the sole controller of your fate. Embrace the boundless potential ahead and allow your RAS-infused voyage to transpire, leading you to a life filled with unparalleled satisfaction, meaning, and delight.

You have the expedition to yourself. Permit your RAS to serve as the ink that molds your extraordinary narrative with audacity.

Books By Sherry Lee:

- ➢ Repeating Angel Numbers
- ➢ Most Popular Archangels.
- ➢ ASKFFIRMATION & AFFORMATION: The Art of Asking and Receiving What You Want and Desire
- ➢ COLLAPSING TIME FOR SUPERNATURAL MANIFESTATION.
- ➢ One Word for a Year or Just a Quarter: Helping your Life and Business to be More Effective.
- ➢ 369 Manifestation Method
- ➢ 66 Ways to be More Productive in the Morning
- ➢ 66 Ways to be More Productive in the Evening.
- ➢ Women Can be Wealthy at Any Age.
- ➢ Streamlining Your Life for Wealth, Abundance, and Prosperity.
- ➢ RAS (Reticular Activating System): How to Use it for Your Highest Good.

Series by Sherry Lee

"Japanese Success Principles"

- ➤ Hansei: The Art of Self Reflection
- ➤ Kaizen: For Continuous Improvement
- ➤ Ikigai: Your True Calling.

"60 Day Devotional"

- ➤ Small Business Devotional
- ➤ Weight Loss Devotional
- ➤ Busy Mom Devotional
- ➤ Busy Dad Devotional
- ➤ MLM Devotional
- ➤ Retired Devotional
- ➤ Student Devotional.
- ➤ Forgiveness Devotional
- ➤ Manifestation Devotional
- ➤ Busy Professional Devotional.

"Laws of the Universe."

- ➤ Laws of Assumption.
- ➤ Law of Vibration
- ➤ Law of Polarity

- Law of Cause & Effect
- Law of Compensation
- Law of Correspondence
- Law of Divine Oneness
- Law of Rhythm
- Law of Perpetual Transmutation of Energy
- Law of Relativity
- Law of Inspiration
- Law of Gender and Gestation
- Law of Reciprocity
- Law of Purpose
- Law of Infinite Possibility
- Law of Unwavering Faith
- Law of Constant Motion
- Law of Analogy
- Law of Free Will
- Law of Expectation/Expectancy
- Law of Increase
- Law of Forgiveness
- Law of Sacrifice
- Law of Obedience
- Law of Non-Resistance
- Law of Action
- Law of Aspiration to a Higher Power
- Law of Charity
- Law of Compassion
- Law of Courage

- Law of Dedication
- Law of Faith
- Law of Generosity
- Law of Grace
- Law of Honesty
- Law of Hope
- Law of Joy
- Law of Kindness
- Law of Leadership
- Law of Non-interference
- Law of Patience
- Law of Praise
- Law of Responsibility
- Law of Self Love
- Law of Thankfulness
- Law of Unconditional Love
- Parkinson's Law.

"Spiritual Attraction."

- Ask, Believe, Receive.
- Faith Like a Mustard Seed.
- You Were Made for Such a Time as This.
- Let Go and Just Let God Handle it for You.
- You Have Not Because You Ask Not.
- Not my Will, Lord but Let Your Will be Done.

- ➢ Asking for This or Something Better.
- ➢ What is your Why.
- ➢ God said 365 Times in the Bible; DO NOT BE AFRAID.
- ➢ 10, 100, and 1,000 Fold Increase.
- ➢ Immeasurable More than I Can Hope or Imagine.
- ➢ All Things are Possible If you Believe.

"Opening and Balancing Your Chakra's"

- ➢ Unblocking your 3rd Eye
- ➢ Opening and Balancing your Heart Chakra
- ➢ Opening and Balancing your Crown Chakra
- ➢ Opening and Balancing your Throat Chakra
- ➢ Opening and Balancing your Solar Plexus Chakra
- ➢ Opening and Balancing your Sacral Chakra
- ➢ Opening and Balancing your Root Chakra.

"Why Alternative Medicine Works"

- ➢ Why Yoga Works
- ➢ Why Chakra Works
- ➢ Why Massage Therapy Works

- Why Reflexology Works
- Why Acupuncture Works
- Why Reiki Works
- Why Meditation Works
- Why Hypnosis Works
- Why Colon Cleansing Works
- Why NLP (Neuro Linguistic Programming) Works
- Why Energy Healing Works
- Why Foot Detoxing Works
- Why Singing Bowls Works.
- Why Tapping Works
- Why Muscle Testing Works.

"Using Sage and Smudging"

- Learning About Sage and Smudging
- Sage and Smudging for Love
- Sage and Smudging for Health and Healing
- Sage and Smudging for Wealth and Abundance
- Sage and Smudging for Spiritual Cleansing
- Sage and Smudging for Negativity.

"Learning About Crystals"

- ➤ Crystals for Love
- ➤ Crystals for Health
- ➤ Crystals for Wealth
- ➤ Crystals for Spiritual Cleansing
- ➤ Crystals for Removing Negativity.

"What Every Newlywed Should Know and Discuss Before Marriage."

- ➤ Newlywed Communication on Money
- ➤ Newlywed Communication on In-laws
- ➤ Newlywed Communication about Children.
- ➤ Newlywed Communication on Religion.
- ➤ Newlywed Communication on Friends.
- ➤ Newlywed Communication on Retirement.
- ➤ Newlywed Communication on Sex.
- ➤ Newlywed Communication on Boundaries.
- ➤ Newlywed Communication on Roles and Responsibilities.

"Health is Wealth."

- ➤ Health is Wealth
- ➤ Positivity is Wealth
- ➤ Emotions are Wealth.

- Social Health is Wealth.
- Happiness is Wealth.
- Fitness is Wealth.
- Meditating is Wealth.
- Communication is Wealth.
- Mental Health is Wealth.
- Gratitude is Wealth.

"Personal Development Collection."

- Manifesting for Beginners
- Crystals for Beginners
- How to Manifest More Money into Your Life.
- How to work from home more effectively.
- How to Accomplish More in Less Time.
- How to End Procrastination.
- Learning to Praise and acknowledge your Accomplishments.
- How to Become Your Own Driving Force.
- Creating a Confident Persona.
- How to Meditate.
- How to Set Affirmations.
- How to Set and Achieve Your Goals.
- Achieving Your Fitness Goals.
- Achieving Your Weight Loss Goals.
- How to Create an Effective Vision Board.

Author Bio

Sherry enjoys devouring and learning through personal development books, so she decided to write about something she is passionate about. More books are coming in series and stand alone because I have learned that I am a very prolific writer averaging about 1 book every 4 days □ Follow me on Amazon for more books.

Thank you for your purchase of this book.

I appreciate and pray for you each and every day.

Thank you, God, Angels, Universe for my wonderful customers.

God Bless You.

Sherry Lee.

Printed in Great Britain
by Amazon

62775817R00077